Upgrade Your Power: The Truth About Attracting Success

By James Fuller

Copyright © 2024 James Fuller

All rights reserved. No part of this book may be used or reproduced by any means, graphic, electronic, or mechanical, including photocopying, recording, taping or by any information storage retrieval system without the written permission of the publisher except in the case of brief quotations embodied in critical articles and reviews.

Cover and Interior Design: Dean Jacobs
www.deanjacobs.com.au

Edited by: Lynda Windsor

Written and Illustrated by James Fuller.

Books may be ordered by contacting:
James Fuller
admin@thecentreforpeace.com.au

Because of the dynamic nature of the internet, any web addresses or links contained in this book may have changed since publication and may no longer be valid. The views expressed in this work are solely those of the author and do not necessarily reflect the views of the publisher, and the publisher hereby disclaims any responsibility for them.

ISBN: 978-1-7638192-0-7

Printed by GT Print.

Preface

> "Success is peace of mind, which is a direct result of self-satisfaction in knowing you made the effort to become the best of which you are capable."
> *Coach John Wooden*

I've had the privilege of helping raise and teach thousands of young people. While my own life has been filled with both challenges and unique experiences, this booklet isn't about me. It's about equipping you with insights, tools, and strategies for building a powerful, successful, and truly fulfilling life.

Over the last 15 years, I've dedicated myself to understanding the complex systems that shape our lives, and one of the profound things I have realised is that life doesn't have to be the way I was raised to see it; I do not have to do life the way others expect me to.

This booklet distills what I've learned from studying the gaps and deficiencies in the personal, social, and global systems that impact us all. The most profound gap in human experience I found is that we do not know "what" we are or "why" we exist; everyone is guessing. Which provides you the power to stamp your thoughts and feelings on the matter… Isn't that cool? This is true power! "The world is your oyster," so, they say.
To make your opinions and observations really matter, to

manifest the things you desire and live a powerful life. Define what you want, aim big, make a plan, go hard... Genius is habit. Genius is as genius does. No thinking required. That's what pure confidence can create. You must understand the structures around you and within you to achieve this type of confidence and find a flowing state in your life. This booklet is here to guide you in navigating these systems wisely, allowing you to achieve freedom and strength, even when you're surrounded by other peoples' limitations.

Political, economic, religious, educational, and social systems—while complex—serve a variety of purposes. Some elements may appear to reinforce established power hierarchies, while others strive toward greater inclusion and support for individuals. Understanding both aspects can help you navigate these structures and find opportunities within them. Unfortunately, we often see that underprivileged individuals are blocked from realising their potential, as these systems may not favour those who don't fit neatly within specific policies, regulations, or criteria for support. If, as an individual, you find you're not achieving your goals, that is a good time to reach out and take a collaborative approach. One of the major challenges in joining forces with others who seek empowerment within these systems is establishing trust. Everyone wants control in some way, and if we allow that to happen, we are simply puppets until we die:

Upgrade Your Power: The Truth About Attracting Success

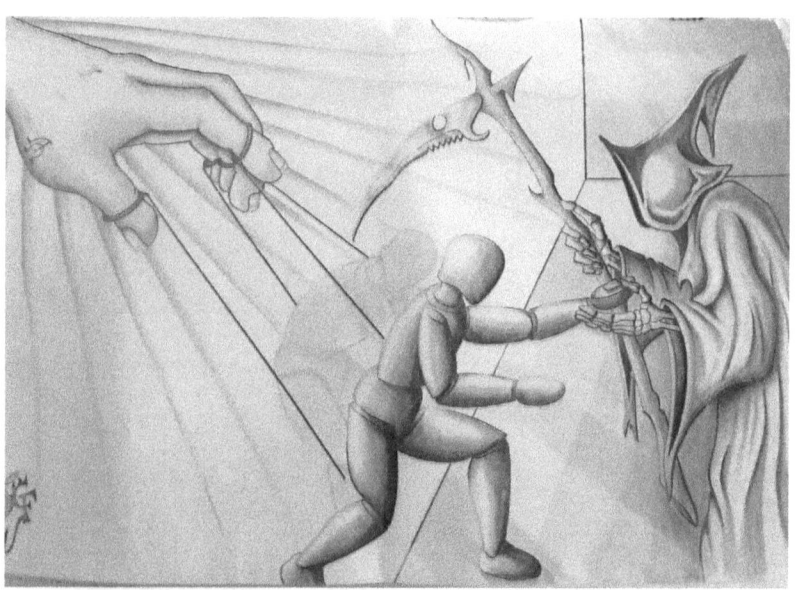

Who truly rules the world? Is it a person, a document, a consortium of corporations, or powerful families? If we knew, do you think they would last long under the scrutiny? What's clear is that poverty, modern-day slavery, and systemic corruption still prevail. If we are born into a world that forces us to abide within any system that does not provide for our basic needs, then something is drastically wrong... Unfortunately, these realities are by design, perpetuated by those who profit from them. So, knowing we must have order in society, which requires rules and regulations, what does true freedom really look like? What do you tell yourself to feel an abundant sense of freedom?

Abraham Maslow gave us one of the most profound models in history – the hierarchy of needs. I often imagen what the world could be if the basic needs of human life were fulfilled in a healthy way. Maslow had a solid grasp on the concept of human potential:

> **"The fact is that people are good, if only their fundamental needs are satisfied, their potentials actualized, and their lives integrated and harmonized."**

Preface

The languages of the powerful and the common person remain worlds apart, and overcoming this disparity is a challenge every individual must confront. The perfect example of this is the design of the education system. It is like an opencut mine. Each school may produce one or two diamonds that go on to be faceted/groomed for positions of power. The remainder are left to slave away in day-to-day jobs keeping the world turning for no real reason other than to keep it turning. What does it take for those low in literacy and talent to have a perfectly wonderful life? Remember, no one is coming to save you; you've got to build your own game plan. No one will live your life for you. We are all victims of our environment. Much of our life is predetermined by the culture we are born into. There is no escaping the bubble—the more we test the limits the more the bubble expands—but the very moment you become aware of this, you can rise above and start building your own destiny, intentionally expanding and strengthening your bubble.

"I am the master of my fate, I am the captain of my soul."
(**Invictus** - by William Ernest Henley)

I'd add: 'within the constraints of the natural laws, the environment and available resources'. With all this in consideration we are all quite powerful people, if we embrace life. I call this 'life by design.'

If you were born into privilege—with safety, access to healthy food, loving people around you and quality resources—you're already ahead of most. Regardless of your starting point, the critical question remains: *how can I leverage what I have?* And the most accurate answer is *choosing goodness*. For those of you who were born into poverty, it will be harder than it is for others; with some smart decisions, grit and collaboration, things will improve significantly.

These are the ideologies that kept me going forward when I was homeless and felt disenfranchised from society:

> "Although the world is full of suffering, it is also full of the overcoming of it."
> Helen Keller

> "Hard times create strong men. Strong men create good times. Good times create weak men. And weak men create hard times."
> Gregory Michael Hopf

> "I don't know what I don't know; so, who does?"

> "Problems are only problems if I make them a problem."

With all my heart, I urge you to liberate yourself from the web of systems that trap well-meaning people, such as the endless cycles of health systems, unfair justice systems, financial debt, outdated education, voting mechanisms, and taxing structures. These systems exist, in part, to keep you bound, busy, and divided from wealth and others seeking a successful life. Goodness is what will set you free. I hope throughout this booklet you will get a sense of goodness and the information about how to set your life up to be as free as possible, with as much adversity required to bring about satisfaction, peace and great happiness. If you feel weak, hopeless, anxious and defeated, then remind yourself that you are the embodiment of love; your literal being is love experiencing itself and that energy that is deep in your bones—the really good stuff—that is worth fighting for... and knowing what I know now, if had I loved myself more I could have avoided many problems.

There is immense potential for true peace, harmony, and balance within the bounds of nature; achievable for those who can reframe their perspective beyond corruption, greed and selfishness. It is known by many names: Utopia, Jesus, Enlightenment, Qi,

Preface

The Great Spirit, The Force, God, Universal Energy, or simply Integrity. No single name captures Its essence, but as more people embrace this understanding, we can gradually free the world from unnecessary adversity. For this to occur society must:

1. Promote critical thinking, preventative health, freedom and empathy in education

2. Fix inequality and economic injustices

3. Strengthen global cooperation and correct governing systems and legislation to be equitable and fair

4. Provide an equitable voice to groups based on their population size. Everyone deserves representation. Currently, we dedicate months of celebrations to minority groups, such as Indigenous communities and Pride celebrations. Yet, the most fundamental figures in existence—mothers and fathers—are celebrated with only a single day each. What about Jesus or love itself? They, too, are acknowledged for just one or two days of the year. This imbalance highlights significant flaws in our governments and the influence of mainstream media, which bears responsibility for many of our ongoing societal issues.

If minority groups aim to enhance their influence and drive meaningful change, they might consider building alliances with larger groups who share mutual interests and offer support. It's also worth recognising that many people are more receptive to understanding different perspectives when approached with respect and openness, rather than feeling that ideologies are being forced upon them.

Upgrade Your Power: The Truth About Attracting Success

None of this is difficult when we have a truly benevolent leadership; which brings the focus back to point 1, and the aim of this booklet.

As you read this booklet, I recommend grabbing a highlighter. Mark anything that resonates with you deeply, then review those highlighted sections again. Discuss these ideas with those in your circle who are also striving for a life of true power and success.

As I write, I reflect on whether my thinking may be too ideological. I'm also mindful of any potential for privileged bias and the possibility of treading on others' ideas. I do so gently, as I have no desire to disrupt anyone's dreams. I have also done my best to refrain from pontificating and instead I have focused on simplifying the process of transmogrification for all who read. Yes, I intentionally used some big poignant words. Look some up; you'll sound smarter!

Provide an equitable voice to groups based on their population size. Everyone deserves representation. Currently, we dedicate months of celebrations to minority groups, such as Indigenous communities and Pride celebrations. Yet, the most fundamental figures in existence—mothers and fathers—are celebrated with only a single day each.

What about Jesus or love itself? They, too, are acknowledged for just one day a year. This imbalance highlights significant flaws in our governments and the influence of mainstream media, which bears responsibility for many of our ongoing societal issues.

If minority groups aim to enhance their influence and drive meaningful change, they might consider building alliances with larger groups who share mutual interests and offer support. It's also worth recognising that many people are more receptive to understanding different perspectives when approached with respect and openness, rather than feeling that ideologies are being forced upon them.

Acknowledgement:

For all the people I have helped and will help in this world: Oh, and Mum, thank you for everything… This is for you.

Upgrade Your Power: The Truth About Attracting Success

By James Fuller

Introduction: The Power of Attraction

Have you ever walked into a room and felt like everyone noticed you, even without saying a word? That's power; not just from your presence, but from who you are and what you radiate. Attracting powerful people—those who can shape your life in incredible ways—isn't about magic or luck. It's about personal development and aligning yourself with principles that naturally draw others toward you.

True attraction isn't about what you own; it's about how you carry yourself. Powerful people notice those who live with intention, those who act from a place of purpose and self-respect rather than passive consumption. I've learned to focus on building myself up, recognising that you can't pour from an empty cup. I used to give and give until I had nothing left myself, then someone pointed out to me that we rarely see mega rich people volunteering or giving their money to the needy, it happens but it's rare in my world.

As much as I've wanted to lift others up, my journey wasn't

Introduction: The Power of Attraction

one of privilege. A few extra breaks—like being helped with the purchase of a car for work, or rent during tough times—could have made all the difference. Yet, it's through overcoming those hardships that I've learned the value of self-reliance and resilience.

I am often asked how my wife and I have stayed together for over 25 years, and it's easy to give the cliches: trust, respect, commonalities. But the real answer is more fluid than that. It has everything to do with divine goodness and belief in each other's potential. Our lives always find ways of coming back together and that feels safe and good. It makes sense!

I spent over two decades as a foster carer, started a registered charity organisation, and founded Sunday markets in my community. Along the way, I represented my state and country in various sports, taught high school English for over 10 years, coached business owners, developed a mobile phone application, and helped many people overcome their fears and build their strengths. During my journey I lost my amazing sister and many close friends to illness and sickness. I also never found out the reason my father abandoned me and remains estranged. These adversities taught me lessons I wish I never had to learn. Even so, they revealed the importance of self-reliance and the necessity of building yourself up before you can make a meaningful difference in the world. I also learnt who I want to attract into my life: more tolerant people who listen and are willing to critically reflect. I am blessed now, surrounded with so many caring, tolerant, peaceful and wise people. I no longer have to slave for others if I do not wish to, and that is an amazing feeling.

With few exceptions, modern "influencers" have little to offer in this challenging world. In fact, much of what they say doesn't apply to my life. While modern thinkers often repackage familiar wisdom, my goal is to go beyond the clichés, offering insights that are both original and practical. They have become so caught up in the fame and economics that they lose touch with what truly matters. Like most successful people, they end up wanting more power and money. Many sell their souls in the name of progress and riches; others do so to feel powerful. I think about this often and, although I don't know the ins and outs of their lives, I can imagine the troubles their profile status attracts. Sure, I would love some of their talent, after all, I've never met a conman I don't like. Access to their resources would be handy—I could do some great things—but I believe after a quick chat with any of them, many would want to trade their lives for mine, while I would not want to trade my life for theirs. There is not a super famous person on the planet that I would trade places with, and that makes me powerful.

Those who are successful at selling a product or service have mastered the formula: once a customer pays, they're committed to making their investment work, and that initial spark of confidence can make any strategy seem effective. Almost any self-help book can achieve the same result if people commit to the changes it offers. If you're searching for yet another repackaging of ancient wisdom, you won't find it here.

Introduction: The Power of Attraction

In this booklet, you can expect original thinking that pushes beyond the motivational clichés. You can expect quotes from powerful sources without the messy interpretations or manipulations that you get from most motivational speakers and modern psychologists. My aim is to inspire you, not manipulate or persuade you. For me, wisdom is about navigating experiences to achieve the ultimate outcomes, which means developing the skills to apply the best knowledge in important situations – This is one of the hardest things anyone can do consistently.

Several times throughout my writing career I have been accused of trying to squeeze too much information into my work. My honours supervisor once said to me my thesis idea would only just fit into a doctorate. One editor for this booklet said plainly "each chapter could be an entire book." Such observations leave me wondering if people will come back to my booklet, or if it will be too overwhelming for you, the reader. My solution is to prewarn you that this booklet is quite dense with information because that's how I like to learn, and I truly wish I had a book like this when I was 17-years-old.

While my chapter entries are short enough to digest, they are full enough to emphasise all the important things for a truly successful life. I highly recommend taking a couple of weeks break between reading each chapter. Use this time to start a challenge, write in your diary, confirm what you're reading, discuss topics with others or reach out to me if you feel that I can help.

You may not know who the people are that I quote within this booklet, but please take the time to look them up. They are iconic people from our past who truly made a difference to millions of lives, and in some cases, the structures of society and even thinking itself.

Whilst your attitude is of the utmost importance to your level of joy and success in life, I'm here to offer you fresh insights that will truly elevate your journey toward success, and ultimately, peace! I am a functional realist and want to give you the applicable tools that you require to develop character, be wealthy and well-loved in this crazy-beautiful world.

Living honourably would have to be the most appealing way of life we understand. To honour the gift of life, it's crucial to focus on the basics that define human decency. Use your manners, offer to help without expecting anything in return, apologise when you're wrong, maintain your integrity and give people gifts simply to show kindness. Love your family and friends as best you can, be silly with them, tell them why you love them, because love is one way, we honour life as the pinnacle of our existence, and it's these small but powerful acts that elevate us. Did you know that the word 'family' literally means "to serve?"

As you build your personal power, remember that enduring strength lies in understanding the frameworks around you. Many consider there to be an illusion, a matrix, a paradox or a problem to solve. I have my thoughts but we won't be discussing these things here. By knowing how systems can impact you, you empower yourself to make choices that align with freedom and purpose. How you behave and treat others will have more impact on your life than what you say, although language is the most

Introduction: The Power of Attraction

profound tool that we have access to; and this is where things become complicated for most people, and why great thinkers thought, and scribes scribed.

Don't be scared to look back at the masters of thinking for yourself; there is no repackaging required when you seek out the greatest minds in history. There are many standouts that deserve their place in history, especially those who discuss the inward journey of life such as the three great dead dudes (you'll find them if you're looking). Please, seek them out and enjoy the fruits of their thoughts. As Marcus Aurelius once said:

"You have power over your mind—not outside events. Realise this, and you will find strength."

So, as you begin this journey to attract power, remember that it begins within! A *stoic* mindset is something we should all be striving for. Definitely Google that man if you don't know what stoicism is.

There are too many giants within our history books to admire in a single lifetime, so, be selective in your approach.

Chapter 1:
The Unspoken Language – Hygiene, Appearance and Awareness

But a powerful mind is only part of the equation. How you present yourself to the world matters just as much. The way you carry yourself—your appearance, your habits, and your respect for yourself and others—creates an immediate impression that can open or close doors. You can attract or repel people simply with your vibe, your energy, and your mindset. Isn't that powerful? Beyond appearance, your inner energy—the confidence, warmth, and focus you radiate—creates a magnetic effect that draws like-minded people toward you while subtly repelling those who don't align with your goals. When you are mindful of this, you can shape the environment around you by embodying the qualities you wish to attract. I use this energy intentionally every day.

They say clothes maketh the man, but let's be real, clothes are not the only things; they are simply one of the most important things, because first impressions matter and the brain judges people before we can blink. It's a safety mechanism that we all have. You wouldn't show up to a job interview wearing pyjamas, right? Your hygiene and appearance are the first things people notice, and it's not just about looking good; it's about respect, for yourself, and for those around you.

Upgrade Your Power: The Truth About Attracting Success

Every little thing you do to show respect will work in your favour. Using your manners, taking your hat and shoes off inside, offering to help, tidying up, no swearing (even if others do), drink minimal or no alcohol and using eye contact is the golden rule in most civilised communities around the world… Show your world that you respect yourself and have the self-discipline to be successful will not go unnoticed. In my family, we have a saying: 'Look good, smell good, feel good'. Just looking after yourself is respectful to others, it shows them that they are worth the effort. As the legendary Coco Chanel put it:

> **"Dress shabbily and they remember the dress; dress impeccably and they remember the woman."**

Whether it's keeping your skin clean, your breath fresh, or your hair neat, these small efforts speak volumes about who you are. People are drawn to those who look like they've got their act together. Looking after your appearance doesn't mean buying designer clothes, but it does mean being mindful of how you present yourself.

Preventative measures play a key role here, too. Cleanliness isn't just about looking sharp; it's about taking care of your overall health and well-being. That's why the saying 'cleanliness is next to godliness' resonates so deeply; because looking after yourself is the first step toward living a strong, resilient life.

The Unspoken Language: Hygiene, Appearance and Awareness

If we really narrow it down, eyes, teeth, feet, inner ear, guts, lungs, hands, feet and skin; these parts of your body, when well-cared for, can significantly impact your quality of life. Can you figure out what they all have in common? They are all associated to your sense. Improving your sensory awareness by trying new things, practicing what you enjoy and observing everything you love is a sure way to level up your confidence and appeal.

It's also beneficial to know a little about key health topics like the Vagus Nerve, hormones, histamine, probiotics and chakras. On the surface there isn't too much to know about these things to take care of them easily. For example, I was taught to remove all excess water and never put anything smaller than my elbow in my ear. Please DYOR because knowing a little bit about these things can prevent major problems from occurring. You can simply ask ChatGPT for the best ways to take care of these things and you'll see it's pretty easy.

Everything you do well for yourself today can pay off immediately but is more likely to pay off in the future. Sometimes you won't feel stronger, wiser, sexier or more confident until weeks or months after working to be a better person. Please remember this piece of ancient wisdom: "Your life is a marathon, not a short distance sprint."

Upgrade Your Power: The Truth About Attracting Success

Understanding these elements of your health can help you maintain balance and address potential issues before they become larger problems. Here is another popular quote: "If you don't make time for your health now, you'll be forced to make time for your sickness later." A clean, well-kept body, mind, and environment reduces unnecessary stress and keeps you moving forward with energy and confidence.

Just as your physical appearance speaks volumes about who you are, so too does your internal balance. Maintaining hormonal balance—through proper diet, sleep, and stress management—is vital for your well-being. When you take snippets of time for yourself in meditation, prayer, cold showers, reading, watching a sunrise, going for a ride or taking a few deep breaths in a row—when you are putting in the effort to do these things—you will attract like-minded people and those who will help you truly excel.

And don't forget to smile! A genuine smile can enhance your appearance more than any expensive outfit or haircut. It's a simple, free way to project warmth, confidence, and positivity. Smile more, even if it feels forced at first. Fake it until you make it! Being around people who smile and make you smile is a powerful healer, bringing lightness and joy into your life.

While physical appearance matters, it's equally important to take care of your mind. Mental health and emotional well-being are just as critical to how you present yourself. Practicing mindfulness, taking breaks, and staying mentally balanced will keep you feeling and looking your best. Bruce Lee notably said:

"As you think, so shall you become."

How you think and care for yourself determines how the world sees you and therefore, in a world full of distractions, staying disciplined and focused on the things that truly matter is a skill that separates the mediocre from the successful.

I like to leave my fruit bowl in full view so I am reminded to eat healthy, I bring the healthy foods to the front of the fridge and cupboards. I use feng shui to motivate myself and position furniture, ornaments, pictures, colours, shapes, lights and motivational sayings around my home and throughout my life. I do so in order to trigger me to remain focussed and motivated. I aim to arrange my life to include a great deal of spontaneity, humour, art and surprise to keep me spirited and light. I especially position things to prompt me to be better than I was yesterday, even just 1%. I try to put in at least 1% extra effort than I did yesterday and give at least 1% more effort than anyone else is doing. I also tell myself—in those moments when I lack motivation—that I must commit to four minutes' engagement in any task that I do not want to do. Keeping moving is one of the secrets to a long, happy life.

Mini Challenge:
First Impression Experiment:

For the next three days, intentionally dress in a way that makes you feel powerful. Keep a daily journal noting how people react differently to you and how these interactions make you feel. Reflect on the impact of self-respect and confidence in your social interactions.

How has paying attention to your appearance and self-care impacted both the way others see you, and how you feel about yourself? Reflect on how small habits of self-respect build confidence and openness in your interactions:

_____
_____
_____
_____
_____

Chapter 2:
The Power of Silence - Talk Less, Listen More

There's a reason why we have two ears and only one mouth. Listening is a superpower.

True confidence is hauntingly silent… have you ever heard the saying beware of the quite ones? Most people think that talking makes them seem smarter or more interesting, but here's a secret: quiet people bring unpredictability and an unknown element that is mysterious and intriguing powerful people love good listeners. When you listen more, you learn more. And when you speak, it has a greater impact. Therefore, only speak when it is thoughtful and kind. Some people might think you are strange or weird or both, but what they think of you is none of your business.

Listening is not just about listening; it is about discerning who is worthy of your time. People such as unreliable sources in the media, the drug abusers, the agenda pushers, the naysayers and those who do not have your best interest at heart, are to be ignored. The random stranger with a story to tell, the veteran, the passionate, the high achievers and those who are busy but still find time to invest in you, are to be sincerely listened to, even if they don't always make sense. Over time you will build discernment, which is also a superpower, and many people believe is a true gift.

Bruce Lee reminds us:

"We must absorb what is good for us and reject the rest."

And as Socrates famously said:

"The only true wisdom is in knowing you know nothing."
This doesn't mean you should stay silent forever, but be selective with who you talk with and the words you speak. When you stop talking and allow for silence, you give yourself room to actually engage; to feel. Listening with intent shows intelligence and empathy. Plus, it's often in quiet moments that we can understand what others truly want and need. It gives us time to compartmentalise, which is another superpower: you can Google that one too!

Real power comes from knowledge, but true wisdom comes from learning how to think in ways that bring great rewards into your life; "I think therefore I am" Rene Descartes - successful people usually specialise in a particular school of thought, or industry that causes them to think in particular ways. Your strengths and weakness in particular frames of thinking will generally determine which pathway you take in life, it is strongly related to which style of learner that you are, and which job interests you – engineer, doctor, lawyer, philosopher, comedian, salesman, politician, sportsperson, scientist, educator, artist, inventor, a child, or a combination of all of them. Each of them has different strengths and weaknesses in their thinking. How will you strengthen your thinking game? Perhaps you can get to know a few of these people and see who appeals to you the most… Show some interest in their work and see what character traits jump out at you.

Edward De Bono's "Six Thinking Hats" has become a widely recognised and influential method in modern success strategies – they can fit into the following descriptions:

Analytical Thinking (White + black hats)
• Focus: Breaking down problems, logical reasoning, and structured analysis.
• Includes: Critical thinking, logical thinking, and convergent thinking.

Creative Thinking (Green hat)
• Focus: Generating new ideas, exploring possibilities, and innovation.
• Includes: Divergent thinking, lateral thinking, and abstract thinking.

Practical Thinking (Yellow Hat)
• Focus: Solving real-world problems and applying common sense.
• Includes: Concrete thinking, strategic thinking, and systemic thinking.

Reflective Thinking (Blue hat)
- Focus: Learning from past experiences and regulating thought processes.
- Includes: Reflective thinking and metacognitive thinking.

Emotional and Intuitive Thinking (Red hat)
- Focus: Making decisions influenced by feelings, instincts, and interpersonal awareness.
- Includes: holistic and intuitive thinking

Listening well is a crucial skill, but so is following through on what you hear in effective ways. Following instructions with focus and attention doesn't just help you succeed in a given task; it demonstrates discipline, reliability, and respect for others' expertise. Often, instructions provide a shortcut to mastering a process that someone else has already perfected, saving you from unnecessary mistakes. When you listen closely and apply instructions precisely, you honor both the guidance given and your own commitment to excellence.

Listening isn't just about hearing words; it's about being fully present. Mindfulness helps you stay grounded in conversations and sharpens your focus. When you're not distracted by your phone or anxious thoughts, and use good eye contact, you become a better listener, which makes you more memorable. The ability to leave people feeling amazing about themselves is a worthy skill worth practicing. Being the voice in someone's head is about the most powerful you can become
.

Mini Challenge: Active Listening Day

Choose one day to practice deep listening, responding only with questions or affirmations. Record your observations about how this impacts your understanding of others and how people respond to your silence. Note how these moments enhance your connections.

When you practiced silence and active listening, what changed in your relationships or your understanding of others? Reflect on how intentional listening might strengthen your connections and add depth to your communication:

_____
_____
_____
_____
_____
_____

Chapter 3:
Speak to Inspire - Develop Your Voice and Vocabulary

Ever heard someone speak and felt like they were reading your mind? That's the magic of a well-developed voice and vocabulary. Your voice isn't just about how you sound; it's about how you express yourself. When you find the right words, you can communicate in a way that truly moves people. Reading books is an excellent way to expand your vocabulary, while listening to a wide range of music can deepen your appreciation for different rhythms and harmonies, which you can apply to both your thinking and behaviour. This will help with becoming a better listener too.

Nelson Mandela once said:

> "If you talk to a man in a language he understands, that goes to his head. If you talk to him in his language, that goes to his heart."

Your vocabulary is your toolkit. The more words you know, the better you can articulate your ideas and emotions. It's not about showing off; it's about connecting with people. A well-placed word directed at the right audience can open doors. Asking quality questions to the right people can be a game-changer.

Upgrade Your Power: The Truth About Attracting Success

Instead of telling people how you feel, ask them how they would feel in the same situation. This is a powerful, manipulative device that is also a polite way to get people to see your perspective. Imagine you're passionate about improving mental health resources in your school or community. Instead of venting to friends or complaining online, you could take proactive steps by reaching out to people with the authority and insight to make a difference. For instance, write a thoughtful letter to your school principal asking about their experience, existing resources or even suggesting if they have considered starting a student-led wellness committee. Alternatively, arrange a meeting with a local council member to discuss their plans for any community programs for youth mental health. By asking clear, focused questions to those who can create real change, you are planting "seeds" in the minds of others. You're addressing your concerns constructively, positioning yourself as a leader and opening doors for future opportunities to make an impact. However, be cautioned: asking the right questions to the wrong people can be devastating. For instance, if you have a criminal record from a traumatic history that you do not want someone to know about, you would not go and ask them if they know about your history, would you? This would pique their interest and they would investigate. Or perhaps you ask the council if the trees you have already planted are within council property. I hope you see what I'm saying.

One of the most underrated skills is emotional intelligence: the ability to understand and manage your own emotions whilst empathising with others. Emotional intelligence is a superpower when it comes to building deep connections with people. When you listen with empathy, you're not just hearing words, you're understanding what the other person feels and thinks. This creates trust, which is the foundation for powerful networking.

Dale Carnegie's classic, *How to Win Friends and Influence People*, teaches us that people are drawn to those who make them feel understood. When you speak in particular ways, you can express certain emotions. When emphasising a calm attitude, joy, authenticity and interest in other people, you can inspire many people. Mastering emotional intelligence is not just about feeling more it is about controlling your emotions in times of leadership and when opportunity arises. This will help you form relationships that create opportunities and influence others. One of the keys to mastering emotional intelligence is acknowledging and overcoming anxiety. Anxiety is very healthy and reminds you that you are alive and experience the gift of life, it is often misunderstood and with some reframing can be a powerful emotion. Anxiety is often based on expectations of things that have not happened yet, far beyond our control.

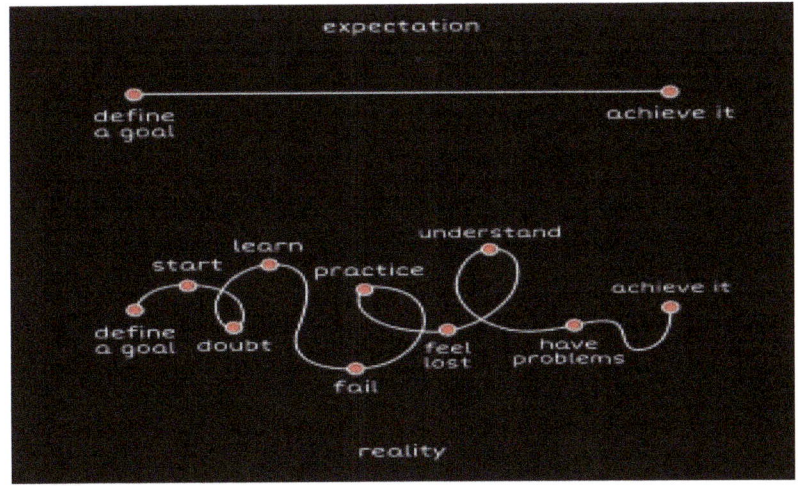

Try to figure out what your expectations are and frame them to be optimistic and positive, change them as required so you maintain composure and demeanor. You'll be amazed at how this can reduce anxiety. I've found that the less anxiety I carry, the more I notice it in others. This could be because I become intimidating as my confidence grows, or just that my focus shifts outward toward others' anxiety, rather than my own. I do this intentionally sometimes to settle my emotions. For highly empathic people, this can be challenging, as empathy makes leaders deeply aware of others' insecurities and can stifle decision making and progress. This is why many powerful individuals are sometimes perceived as more narcissistic: they may not feel others' insecurities as intensely. I'm not suggesting that we should abandon empathy to gain power. Instead, we should seek people who match our awareness and can elevate us. But it's worth noting why power can come more easily to those who are less affected by empathy, echoing J.R.R. Tolkien's sentiment:

"Those who desire power are not fit to hold it!"

Ideal power stems from adoration; people genuinely liking you and wanting you as their leader. Learning to communicate your abilities and intentions authentically puts you in the best position to gain true influence.

Words are powerful. They can be twisted, rearranged, and framed to make almost any argument persuasive; that's why the narrative you choose to live by is so critical. The story you tell yourself—and the one you project to the world—can either limit your potential or unlock it. Be mindful of the words you use, both internally and externally, because they have the power to shape your reality. The narrative you embrace can hinder or propel your life toward success and empowerment. I believe the most powerful narrative is one that convinces your psyche that it is necessary for you to achieve or do something specific. The very moment you believe something is necessary your emotions solidify, and you become unwavering. Therefore, tell yourself a narrative that convinces you on the deepest levels possible that your goal is **necessary.**

Developing your voice isn't just about what you say—it's about how you think. Creativity plays a huge role here. Great communicators don't just recite facts—they find innovative ways to express ideas. Whether it's through writing, art, or speaking, let your creativity flow and use it to inspire others.

In addition to expanding your vocabulary and sharpening your message, it's crucial to develop your physical voice. Your voice is not just the words you use; it's how you deliver them. The tone, pitch, and volume all play a role in how others perceive you. A well-developed voice commands attention and projects confidence. A voice can impact a nervous system.

Practice breathing techniques, posture, and vocal exercises to strengthen your voice, ensuring that it resonates with power and clarity. As Vin Giang says,

"Your voice is your instrument"—the better you play it, the more effectively you'll inspire and influence others."

Learning to speak in front of crowds is one of the most powerful skills you can develop. Confidence comes from preparation and practice. The more you do it, the easier it becomes. Command the room by believing in your message, standing tall, and speaking with purpose. People are drawn to confidence, and your ability to project that confidence in public will set you apart.

Mini Challenge: 30-Second Message

Create a short, impactful message on a topic that inspires you. Practice it until it flows naturally. Share this message with someone and ask for feedback on its clarity and impact, noting how it feels to use your voice purposefully.

How did preparing and delivering a short speech affect your confidence in expressing yourself? How do you feel inspiring others? Consider how refining your voice and vocabulary could empower you in meaningful conversations:

_____
_____
_____
_____

Chapter 4:
Surround Yourself with Proactive People—Energy is Contagious

One of the most difficult things a person can do is choose their friends. We are so often pushed into situations that oblige us to be friendly and one thing leads to another. If this happens at work or in a club it can be difficult to tell people you don't want to be friends… simply giving very short answers or politely suggesting that you cannot help at this moment works most of the time. I don't show interest in their stories I fidget when they talk to me, I use less eye contact, I don't offer to help them unless it's super important. All the things that we shouldn't do if we want to make friends. I used to say yes to everyone and try to be friends with everyone, unfortunately I was too successful, and I ended up being used and abused. There are 4 types of friends based on how long you can tolerate them: 4-minute friends, 4-hour friends, 4-day friends and 4-ever friends.

Even with a strong voice and vision, your success is profoundly shaped by the company you keep. The energy, ambitions, and attitudes of those around you can either elevate your path or weigh it down. That's why surrounding yourself with proactive, purpose-driven individuals isn't just a strategy; it's essential to reaching new heights. As Jim Rohn famously said,

> "You are the average of the five people you spend the most time with."

This means that you identity is literally shaped by the people around you and we all know how important your identity is. The deepest part of your life, your persona and your character define what and who you are, if you don't believe me try to put that into words: write out what and who you are without using the descriptions that other people have provided (I go into detail about this in my next book). By aligning with people who are positive, motivated, and growth-oriented, you naturally elevate your own standards, habits, and achievements. Your circle shapes your mindset, reinforces your goals, and ultimately determines the momentum of your success.

In the journey toward self-mastery, recognising the influence of larger societal systems is as vital as understanding the energy within your immediate circle. Many of the structures we encounter—whether in education, finance, healthcare or others—weren't necessarily designed with personal empowerment in mind. Learning to navigate them with strategic awareness is key. Sometimes, true power lies in knowing when to challenge these systems, when to work within them, and when to disengage entirely. Surround yourself with people who not only support your goals but also understand the importance of this practical dissent, guiding you to grow beyond the boundaries others have set. Does your teacher help you with this? Your coach? Your doctor? Your broker? Your boss?

Look around—are your friends pushing you to be better, or are they holding you back? Is your workplace supportive of your growth, or are they exploiting your time and hard work? Do you have too many people in your circle?

Upgrade Your Power: The Truth About Attracting Success

Something else to remember is not to be overwhelmed or overly impressed by people who out-perform you. Congratulate them. Smile politely. If the timing is right, ask for their advice. Then mimic them and practice to improve yourself. How you respond to other high performers will get noticed - Mimicry is the highest form of flattery.

When you're surrounded by people who are actively working toward their goals, you'll find yourself inspired to do the same. This becomes the common factor in your relationship and underpins fruitfulness and all the positive traits of a powerful person.

Common sense stems from a functional family, loving relationships, culture and teamwork. Common sense, though often overlooked, is a powerful tool in shaping a successful life. It grounds us, keeps us balanced, and helps us navigate complex situations with clarity and ease. When combined with practical knowledge and self-awareness, common sense becomes an irreplaceable asset. Powerful people recognise potential energy, and they'll notice when you are part of a productive, uplifting network. Imagine building a team like your favorite YouTuber's squad; people who get your vibe and push you to be better, just like how *Supercar Blondie, MrBeast* or *Emma Chamberlain* built their crew. Choose people who fuel your goals, not just hang around. It is common knowledge that if you truly love your job you will never work a day in your life.

Surround Yourself with Proactice People: Energy is Contagious

In fact, being part of a committed team—whether it's a sports team, a marriage, or any close-knit group—can prevent devastating outcomes like depression. Good teams, in any form, provide a support system and foster healthy expectations that anchor us through life's challenges. The depth of a connected relationship, especially with a loving and affectionate partner, profoundly impacts our well-being. Regular intimacy with someone who cherishes you—both physically and emotionally—helps balance hormones, promotes mental clarity, relieves anxiety and offers a sense of bliss and grounding. When shared in an atmosphere of respect and affection, these experiences enhance emotional stability and boost confidence, proving that meaningful connections are essential for a fulfilled life.

While the idea that 'teamwork makes the dream work' emphasises the value of working with others, taking on challenges independently is equally powerful. The best leaders are those who know when to work within a team and when to go solo. Becoming a maverick—someone unafraid to pursue goals alone—builds resilience, creativity, and a unique perspective that enriches the journey toward success. The sentiment that I use in my professional email signature resonates perfectly here: "As an individual succeeds so does a community." Your behaviour literally contributes to the global community and your successes contribute to the collective success of our world. The following image displays the intensity of harmonising with the external world. When you feel good, strong and healthy this is the vibe you will emit into the world. "As within, so without."

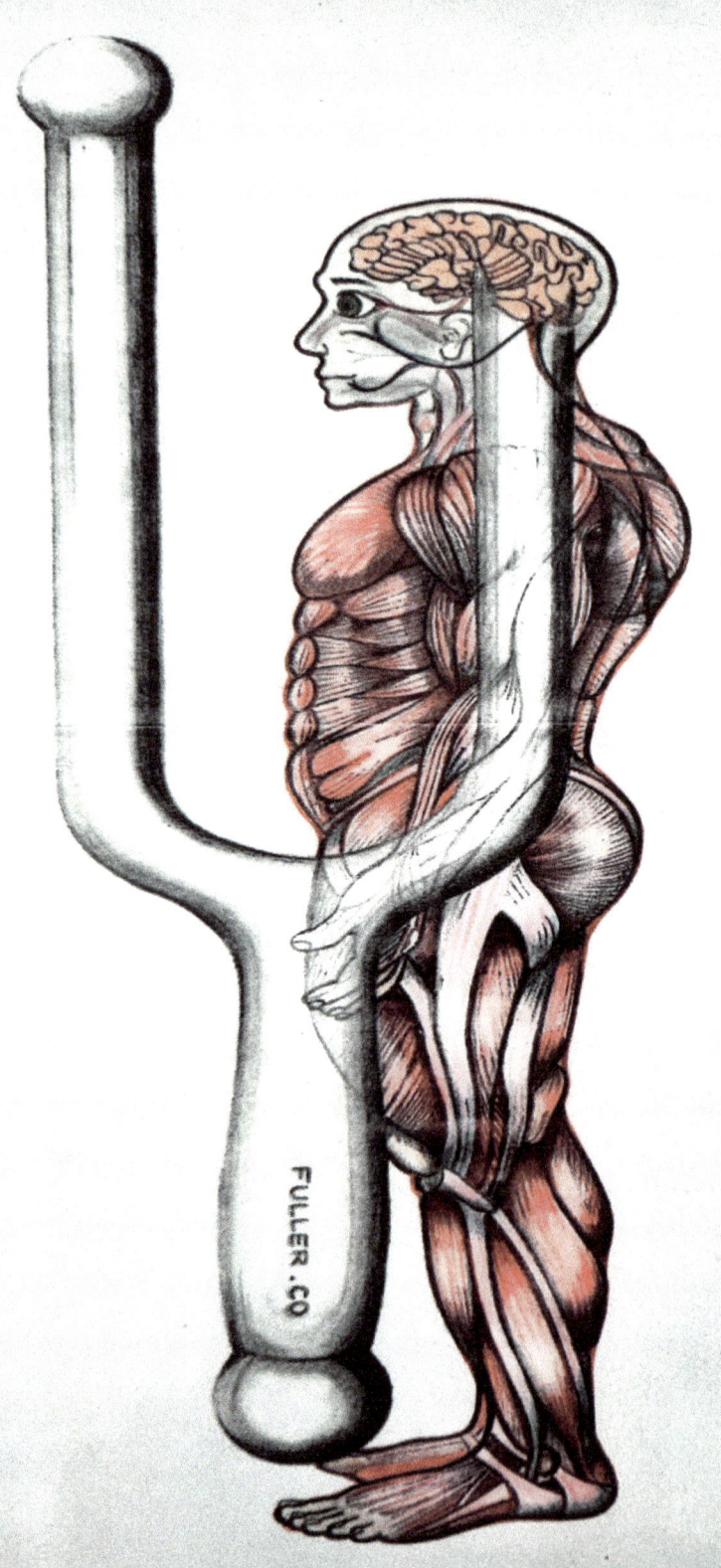

Surround Yourself with Proactice People: Energy is Contagious

Therefore, if I can help refine your approach, my contribution becomes greater too.

Turning up—showing your face consistently—shows commitment, integrity and trustworthiness, but knowing when to strategically withdraw is as equally powerful. Sometimes, absence can be a statement, showing your discernment in where to invest energy and time. Considered withdrawing, as referenced by Johan Galtung, is a strategy to disengage from, or change, systems and people that don't align with your purpose.

You will never become rich and fulfilled simply by working a 9-5 job for people who don't support your wealth goals or inspire you to become your best. Demand more for yourself. Beware of getting caught up in systems, working for the government or large corporations. You may encounter many well-meaning people, but some may unintentionally hold you back, trapped by their own indoctrination and pursuit of success within the same limiting framework.

You may find yourself in limbo quite often until you find the right people with which to surround yourself. In the meantime, embracing diversity—whether it's in culture, background, or opinions—broadens your perspective and helps you grow. When you include different voices in your circle, you gain wisdom from every corner of life. Try volunteering or working in a space that will challenge you… you won't regret it.

Mini Challenge: Network Reflection

List the five people who most influence your mindset. Reflect on how each person contributes to or detracts from your growth. Decide on one action to either increase positive interactions, or distance from negative influences. Set a plan to connect with someone you admire.

After assessing your circle of influence, what have you learned about the impact of others on your mindset and goals? Reflect on how aligning yourself with proactive, positive people could accelerate your personal growth. Make a list of people you need to seek out in your life over the next 12 months:

_____
_____
_____
_____

Chapter 5:
Personal Development - Talent and Exercise

You don't need to be the best at everything, but you do need to be really good at something. Whether it's playing the guitar, coding, or mastering a sport, having a talent sets you apart. People are attracted to those who are passionate and dedicated to their craft. Plus, developing a talent teaches you discipline, which is key to personal growth. Try to remember that you can't do everything, but you can do anything you apply yourself to."

Building skills not only enhances our capabilities but also strengthens our memory and mental agility. Every time we learn something new, we create new neural connections and further develop our capacity for recall. In the long run, this directly shapes our resilience and mental sharpness. Learning is truly a gift that keeps on giving, building our character with each new step.

But don't stop at mental talents—get physical too. Exercise sharpens both our body and mind. "To keep the body in good health is a duty," said the Buddha, and he was right. Physical strength supports mental strength. Whether it's running, lifting weights, or yoga, staying active gives us energy and confidence. And remember, being fit isn't just about daily survival; it's about thriving and enjoying life to the fullest. Our physical health should allow us to engage in life's adventures, whether it's hiking, dancing, or simply having the stamina to keep up with our passions. In fact, learning to dance will also give you an edge throughout life. Movement in general is vital to life: babies will roll around for fun but also to alleviate growing pains and wind. Adults should probably do this more often. Walking and triggering the pressure points on the bottoms of your feet, simply grounding yourself to the natural Earth, and working with your hands all send hyper-rewarding feedback to your brain that tells it to stay alive, thrive and fight off disease, because you have a purpose; jobs to see, places to meet and people to do!

Building survival skills is the most primal pathway to real confidence. It isn't just about navigating the outdoors: it's about strengthening your inner resilience. Training in basic survival tactics—like fire-building, finding safe water sources, trapping a fish, preparing and storing food, orientating yourself using nature's geometry or creating shelter—trains both your body and mind, grounding your confidence in real-world capabilities. These skills activate your nervous system in controlled, challenging ways, helping to build resilience to stress and fostering a deep sense of self-reliance. Through survival skill practice, you teach your body to handle adrenaline and anxiety effectively, preparing you not just for emergencies, but also for any of life's daily stressors. So, what are you waiting for? Find a bushman and ask them to take you out bush with minimal resources. Switch your phone off and only use it in emergencies. Make sure you tell people where you're going and set times to be in contact. The bushman 100% knows these things. If you can't find one, reach out, I can link you in with the best. Learning to survive will give you a sense of freedom deeper than anything else can.

Don't aim for health just to function day to day—aim to fully enjoy your life. Being fit and healthy enough to truly live well means you'll have the energy, vitality, and joy that make life worth living. You will feel the effects of aging soon enough, and that's when the extra effort you put in during your younger years will truly matter.

Developing a talent requires dedication and discipline, but that doesn't mean working endlessly. Everything is so difficult at first, especially getting started, and it's perfectly ok to rest, but resting can become easy too. So be warned! If you feel stuck, then you are, and you need to get moving, because resting can lead to the most difficult obstacle to overcome: starting again!

Smart planning is the key. Plan your attack for today, tomorrow and over your lifetime. Time management is pertinent to your success. Set clear, achievable goals and stick to a schedule that allows time for both work and rest. When you're intentional with your time, you make room for creativity and personal growth.

Upgrade Your Power: The Truth About Attracting Success

Our memory and our character are inseparable. Who we are is built on the memories we choose to keep and the moments we learn from. For instance, getting into trouble as a young person definitely can come back to bite you later on. I applied for weapons license and they pulled up my entire record from 10-years-old. I grew up in the 90's so obviously it was rejected the first time around. Powerful people will want to know you have a relatively clean record, and that you can be trusted. Developing a strong memory isn't just about recalling information; it's about preserving the lessons and relationships that define us. Cultivating memory recall and reinforcing neural pathways is a vital foundation of self-growth and wisdom.

It is important to note that confidence usually stems from reflecting on your past performances. It's about finding inspiration within yourself and occasionally in others' success. Welcoming feedback and offering it to others, can be the difference between success and failure. Kind, supportive, useful feedback is most likely the best advice I have for you in this entire booklet. These are the relationships you want, especially in your marriage, with your teachers, children, parents etc. Surround yourself with inspiring figures, but don't forget to be self-inspired by continuing to try new things, pushing your limits, and celebrating your own achievements. The more you challenge yourself, the more confident you become in your abilities.

Mini Challenge:
Practice Makes Perfect

Choose a skill or talent you wish to enhance, such as public speaking or physical fitness. Dedicate 15 minutes daily for a month, tracking your progress weekly. Reflect on how this commitment influences your confidence and self-discipline. Also, make your bed every day!

What did you notice about your motivation and progress as you practiced a skill or maintained daily physical activity? Reflect on how dedicating time to talents and health could impact other areas of your life:

_____
_____
_____
_____
_____
_____
_____
_____

Chapter 6:
Habits to Avoid

Just as good habits can make you stronger, bad habits can hold you back from becoming the best version of yourself. Here are some common habits to avoid if you want to succeed:

1. Procrastination: Putting things off will only add stress and lower your productivity. Don't put off until tomorrow what you can get done today. Rudyard Kipling reminds us to treasure every moment in his most famous poem, *If:* "If you can fill the unforgiving minute with sixty seconds' worth of distance run, yours is the Earth and everything that's in it".

2. Negative Self-Talk and Anxious Thoughts: If you constantly doubt yourself, you'll never reach your full potential. One of my favourite things to do is help others overcome anxiety; then mine seems to fade off into the background. When my anxiety is at its peak, I remind myself the anxiety is a divine gift; one that allows me to feel extreme feeling and reminds me I am alive. Not everyone can feel as deep as I can and sense what I can sense. Anxiety to me can be a really positive thing.

We are often told that worrying is pointless, and many famous figures have explicitly stated—or alluded to—this idea. But let me tell you: worry is not a wasted emotion. It's a perfectly normal part of love and care. The real danger lies in worrying about worrying—a depressive and dangerous spiral that traps so many people. While less worry can be beneficial, a life without worry isn't realistic or healthy.

Unnecessary worry can be problematic, but how can we ever

truly know what's unnecessary? Embrace your worries, knowing it's entirely natural and even healthy to feel concerned about things that matter deeply to you and impact your life. (And as a helpful reminder, consider the wisdom of the Serenity Prayer.)

Moreover, worry often leads to crying, which has been scientifically shown to be wonderfully therapeutic. Crying is, in my view, one of the most magical and special human experiences. Honestly, I wish I cried more.

3. Toxic Relationships: Surrounding yourself with people who drain your energy will stop you from growing. This just happens to be most people I meet, and it can be difficult to avoid.

4. Comparing Yourself to Others: Everyone's journey is different. Focus on your own path. Just because the carnivore or vegan diets are good for one person, does not mean they are good for you.

5. Neglecting Health: Poor diet, lack of exercise, and not getting enough sleep will slow your progress.

6. Fear of Failure: Being afraid to make mistakes will prevent you from taking the necessary risks for growth. (No one has ever fallen from Heaven a master, we must all learn, which takes education, practice, repetition, application and reflection.). Michael Jordan famously said "I've missed more than 9,000 shots in my career. I've lost almost 300 games. Twenty-six times, I've been trusted to take the game-winning shot and missed. I've failed over and over and over again in my life. And that is why I succeed."

7. Seeking Approval: Don't base your self-worth on what others think. Trust in your abilities. Keep your plans to yourself until they're realised. Be somewhat mysterious: let others witness your results, not just your intentions. A sense of quiet confidence is a magnetic trait that often speaks louder than words.

8. Over-Commitment: Saying yes to everything can spread you too thin. I did this for too many years. I just wanted to have as much fun as I could in any way I could. Prioritise what's important. I realised that being selective is less exhausting, and therefore, more energy becomes available to have fun.

9. Lack of Focus: Constant distractions and multitasking lead to mediocre results. Think about the time you spend scrolling TikTok or Insta. What if even half of that went toward building something awesome for yourself? Curate your feed to inspire you, not drain you.

10. Ignoring Feedback: Learn from constructive criticism and use it to improve. Fredrick Nietzsche implied we may all seem a bit mad to those who can't hear the music we're dancing to. Therefore, be selective in seeking feedback, and acknowledge unsolicited feedback politely. It might still hold something useful. I have learnt a great deal in robust discussion with good people. Just because we think and believe something deeply does not make us correct or accurate... be sceptical of others, and yourself! Reflect on your own thoughts and beliefs to consider if you're wrong! This will identify weaknesses and allow you to build your strengths. One of my favourite mantras is "Am I wrong."

11. Don't be too silent: Strategic silence can be a superpower, but don't stay quiet if something doesn't feel right, or if you need clarity on something important to you. Raise your voice, speak up, lobby for change, and appeal to the common sense of those around you; after all, the world could use a lot more common sense. As Edmund Burke said, "The only thing necessary for the triumph of evil is for good men to do nothing". Misplaced anger can harm your reputation, but well-directed and principled anger can earn you deep respect from powerful

Habits to Avoid

people. If you feel unheard, seek other avenues while reflecting on whether this battle truly deserves your time and energy.

12. Avoid identifying as something you are not: Authenticity is the key to attracting genuine power. If you spend too much time associating with minority groups (even if you are in one) or trying to fit into identities that don't align with your core, you risk being distracted from the goals that truly matter to you. With minority groups often come great struggles, which may limit your capacity to draw in powerful people who can propel you forward. Focus your energy on growth and progress that aligns with your natural strengths and ambitions. If your minority group is your passion and you wish to create a freedom movement, then you can expect a lot of hard work ahead of you. All the best…

13. Reliance on technology: Cybersecurity and automation are hot topics right now. Our future seems to be riddled with self-driving, self-creating, self-analysing everything, but what it can never do is humanise, self-reflect, comprehend and feel emotions, comprehend nuanced language, create original artworks without human input, be intuitive, learn from personal experiences, exercise freewill, learn from complex social environments, provide genuine human companionship; and there are more. You get my point. AI has its place as a tool—a very powerful tool if you know how to use it—and it can replace you in many ways, but if you get stuck comparing yourself to AI, in fear of it or in awe of its capabilities, you will end up sick and lose any power that you have built. One of the most damaging habits you can develop is constantly comparing yourself to others, especially on social media. So, don't do that. Remember, people often show only the highlights of their lives online, not the struggles or imperfections. While occasionally we see something inspiring, much of the content online is fake. Comparison robs you of joy and slows your progress. Focus on your own journey and seriously give your best at every turn. Distance yourself from screen time: While you're watching stories or other people live their lives, your life is slipping by. Use that time instead to engage with the world directly, to pursue your own passions, and to build meaningful connections. If you measure your success against others, you'll never feel like you're enough. Instead, strive to be the best version of yourself and disconnect from the need for validation through likes and follows.

14. The News and Media: If it's irrelevant to you don't let it bother you. Most of what you see in the media is lies, non-truths and manipulation. Even the people you want to trust are manipulating you to see their worldview and take your money or consume your time in some way. What is happening in other countries, in politics, sport and other 'important' topics is ALWAYS construed to suit the agenda of the people who own the media. It cannot be trusted. I engage with these things as little as possible and I certainly do not allow politics, religion or the media to sway my way of thinking or impact my life: that, my friends, is for weak individuals.

Avoiding *unnecessary stress* is a key to success. All these habits to avoid are literal gateways to drugs and alcohol abuse which are major problems with memory function. Our memory is the utmost beautiful thing about being human and I hope you will embrace habits to improve your memories and recall. Steer well clear of anything that will reduce your lung capacity or wreck your stomach biome. The stability in each of these places is vital to your stress response.

While some stress can be motivating, unnecessary stress can sap your energy and focus. In fact, stress is the biggest killer on the planet, but it is also poorly understood. When we think about it, stress underpins almost all our problems, but it also motivates us to move and complete tasks. I divide stress into necessary and unnecessary adversity.

Upgrade Your Power: The Truth About Attracting Success

Learning when to say "no", how to delegate tasks, and create healthy boundaries for yourself is mandatory to a successful life, especially when you can feel at peace with these things. Creating healthy boundaries is something we are rarely taught in schools. You should research this… or message me for an introduction to setting boundaries. However, remember that adversity builds character! It's through overcoming challenges that you develop resilience, strength, character and wisdom. So, choose your battles wisely and remain focused on overcoming the necessary adversity to achieve your main goals. While I don't like the schooling system much, being able to sit still and complete your work as best you can, overcoming any difficult calculations or struggles you have will form the person you will become. Some form of specialised schooling is a 100% necessary adversity to meet in order to be successful and powerful in life. One thing I can recommend for helping your school life to become a bit easier is to identify which way you prefer to learn. Do you find it easier to learn when talking, listening, watching, reading or doing? Discuss this with your teacher… If they are not supportive of your needs or offer a suitable compromise, definitely find a new teacher/coach/educator. Either way, do your best at school and if it's too hard, tell someone in power and ask for a personalised program; staff are there to serve your genuine needs and see you succeed. Or, call me and I will talk to your school for you.

Life will throw challenges your way and much of it you may classify as unnecessary adversity: frustration, pain, exhaustion, and sometimes things simply won't go according to plan no matter how hard you try. But you will have this wisdom: **be prepared!** Here's a truth that's often overlooked: learning to remain calm, seeing the humour in life, staying light-hearted, and not taking everything personally is an underrated superpower. When you laugh at yourself and find the humour in difficult situations, you gain perspective and an incredible sense of inner freedom. Humour allows you to distance yourself from negativity and judgment and see that not everything is worth taking so seriously.

> **"Do not take life too seriously.
> You will never get out of it alive."**
> - Elbert Hubbard

Being funny or light-hearted doesn't mean you're avoiding responsibility; it means you're resilient enough to face challenges with a smile. As the saying goes, 'Don't sweat the small stuff, and it's all small stuff.' When you don't let insults or criticism get to you, you develop a kind of emotional armour. You become immune to pettiness and rise above negativity to maintain some positive focus. Unnecessary adversities are all around us and if we distance ourselves from negative environments, people, systems and behaviours, we make smart choices. We establish a bubble around us that protects us from idiots, dumbness, stupidity and purposeless work.

People are drawn to those who can laugh and bring joy into a room. It's a form of confidence, knowing that you are secure in who you are and that no external comment or insult can shake you. And more than that, humour connects us. It lightens the mood, brings people together, and reminds us that, even in the face of adversity, life is still beautiful and worth enjoying. So, don't forget to practice banter and develop some inside jokes with your mates. Then combine this with all the reading you've been doing, the habits you've been avoiding and the jobs you've been completing, and you will start to attract other powerful people.

Mini Challenge: Digital Detox

For the next 48 hours, limit your social media use to 30 minutes per day. Use the extra time to focus on something productive or relaxing. Or

Identify a habit you want to avoid (e.g., procrastination or negative self-talk). Spend the next week replacing this habit with a positive behavior. Keep a daily log of how it affects your mindset and productivity, observing changes over time.

*You could always try 8 days without alcohol or coffee.

What insights did you gain by observing or reducing a habit that no longer serves you? Reflect on how letting go of unhelpful habits could create space for more empowering behaviors in your life. Make a plan:

_____
_____
_____
_____
_____

Chapter 7:
Be the First to Recover: Avoiding Trauma and Crisis

Life is unpredictable. No matter how well you plan or how much you try to steer clear of trouble, trauma and crisis can strike when you least expect it. The key to long-term success is not just about avoiding hardships, but about mastering the art of resilience—bouncing back quickly and stronger than ever. True power isn't just about success; it's about carrying yourself with dignity and grace, especially when times are tough. Maintaining dignity amidst challenges not only strengthens your character, but also reinforces your self-worth and respect from others. Here are a few tips to help you build resilience:

Prevention: Prevention is the great cure! Success comes from staying in alignment with your principles, goals, and emotional health. Consistent self-care creates a strong foundation that helps you navigate challenges effectively. Be proactive: avoid toxic relationships, avoid crises, manage stress, and make decisions that align with your bigger vision. Take care of the things that take care of you. Do the maintenance on your pushbike, and in your relationships. Buying flowers because you love someone is far more powerful than buying flowers to apologise for any problems that arise. Recognising potential sources of crisis before they escalate is essential. If you remain vigilant, you can often sidestep drama before it derails your progress.

Crisis Strikes: Keep Your Head! When the unexpected happens, stay calm. Take a breath, step back, and assess the situation. Trouble never sends a warning and you will be surprised how remaining calm and smiling will fix your problem before you know it. Panicking or reacting emotionally often leads to poor decisions, which only deepens the crisis. As Rudyard Kipling said in his poem If, "If you can keep your head when all about you are losing theirs... yours is the Earth." The ability to keep your cool when others crumble is your greatest strength in times of crisis.

One of the hardest things a person can do is wait; apply time. After doing everything you can, applying patience can be extraordinarily difficult. Learning how to play chess is a terrific way to manage these emotions; poker can help a little too. What you do during the waiting time to curb self-sabotage or avoid attracting negativities genuinely matters in achieving your goals efficiently. This period requires focus, patience, and the willingness to let time do its work while you maintain your momentum.

Make a list of possible solutions and prioritise what you can control. In moments of confrontation and stress, the natural instinct might be to react quickly, emotionally, or defensively. But here's a secret: calm wins most of the time.

My best mate often says that chess is the game closest to life, not only do we need patience to play but with a finite number of moves on the table, no one knows what move you will make, which is exciting and empowering.

The Serenity Prayer

God, grant me the serenity to accept
the things I cannot change,
Courage to change the things I can,
And wisdom to know the difference.

Remaining calm in stressful situations gives you clarity, control, and the ability to think strategically when others are losing their heads. When you respond with calmness and consideration, rather than react, you disarm hostility and avoid escalating the situation. As Marcus Aurelius said, "The nearer a man comes to a calm mind, the closer he is to strength." Those who can stay grounded amidst chaos become leaders by default, because they project strength and reliability.

Recovery: Rapid Response and Adaptation! Once you've assessed the situation, focus on the solution, not the problem. The quicker you shift into problem-solving mode, the faster you recover. Adaptation is key—use the experience to grow and evolve. Whether it's reworking your plans, seeking help from your network, or taking time to heal, it's important to act fast, but thoughtfully. Channel your energy into rebuilding better and smarter.

Every crisis is a learning opportunity. As you recover, ask yourself: What can I learn from this? What would I do differently next time? This reflection is how you turn adversity into power. Success isn't defined by the absence of challenges, but by how quickly and effectively you recover when they come. Keep your mindset strong, stay grounded, and continue to move forward; because every setback can become the launching pad for your next leap forward.

> "Do not pray for an easy life,
> pray for the strength to endure a difficult one."
> - Bruce Lee

Upgrade Your Power: The Truth About Attracting Success

It's important to recognise that not everything you think is true. In a world filled with scammers, tricksters, and misinformation, adopting a mindset of healthy skepticism is essential. It's not about doubting everything, but about critically assessing the information that comes your way. Once you've been sceptical and done your due diligence, then you can stand tall with confidence - when we remove all doubt, we become powerful.

Don't believe things at face value quite often all the options being presented to you are second rate. You risk becoming a passive consumer which, in my opinion, is highly ranked as the worst life a human can have; Question, research, and think independently, do your due diligence and you will get the rewards and avoid many unnecessary adversities.

For example, the word 'gratitude' is currently trending, and I genuinely dislike this word. I investigated the true meaning of this word, and I believe gratitude is an unhealthy practice that weakens the mind and distracts from true love, sincere thankfulness and connection. It is often confused with other words that trick people into obligation to give a gift and feel or behave a certain way. Another word I believe is a farcical manipulative tool is "ego." For starters, no one can tell me where it is in the body or what it really is, but some illusionary 'thing' causes us to have an inflated sense of self. The media use it to make you feel guilty and belittled every time you are focused on developing and performing based on self-interest, which is generally very healthy. I am not one to fall for the convincing trip into the manipulative world of "ego," a manufactured nonsensical psychological zeitgeist that shifts every few years to keep people watching the media like they would a candle in a dark room. "Wake up" is another problematic term. Don't all these redundant terms simply mean don't be narcissistic and self-absorbed but expand your awareness about life so you can achieve more and help others find peace too?

Vulnerability is an often-overlooked quality that forms a critical part of strength. We are all vulnerable. We are all on a learning curve of expanding our awareness. Being open about struggles, fears, or mistakes fosters connection with others and reveals the depth of our courage. True resilience isn't just about appearing strong; it's about showing authenticity, even in difficult times. Although, deciding who we can trust to share our vulnerabilities with is often a difficult decision.

Healthy skepticism is a shield that protects us from being misled and helps us make informed decisions in a world riddled with deception. Who can you trust? What information can you trust? Now, they are two enormously important questions. Simply because someone opens up to you does not mean you can trust them. Or just because the news makes sense does not make it the truth. The capacity for self-reflection and the ability to acknowledge when you are wrong will supercharge your relationships and your self-worth. Be skeptical about people and information: all smart people do this.

It goes for your own personality too. Have you ever considered if you are a narcissist, a sociopath, the ignorant one or the common variable in the problems all around you? Now that you have this skill of maintaining a skeptical mind, it's essential to also trust where trust is warranted.

So, use your common sense and healthy scepticism as your greatest allies in avoiding crises. In a world full of misinformation, common sense is often a guiding light, helping you evaluate decisions with clarity. A healthy scepticism questions the motives behind advice, challenges popular beliefs, and ensures that we're not misled by appearances or persuasive marketing. Combining common sense with critical thinking keeps you anchored, no matter the situation.

Mini Challenge: Crisis Plan Simulation

Simulate a minor crisis (e.g., managing a difficult conversation). Write out three calm, productive ways to respond. Practice these strategies and evaluate how this simulation prepares you for real-life situations. Reflect on the importance of calm and strategy in crisis.

What did simulating a potential crisis teach you about your capacity for resilience and clear-headedness? Reflect on how adopting a proactive mindset can help you navigate real-life challenges with greater confidence:

_____
_____
_____
_____

Chapter 8:
Believe in Something Greater: Define Your Purpose

There are many truths in the world, but the only genuine Truth is the one you fully believe in with your body, mind, and spirit. The beliefs you hold shape your reality and determine the actions you take. If you don't stand firmly in your own truth, you allow the world to define it for you. Choose your beliefs carefully, and once you find a truth that resonates, live by it fully. That commitment will guide your decisions and help you overcome doubt and confusion.

Albert Einstein said:

> "The value of a college education is not the learning of many facts but the training of the mind to think."

The essence of a real education is to learn to navigate the complexities of life and cultivate an ability to think critically, make informed choices, and define our meaning and purpose.

To become truly powerful, you need to believe in something greater than yourself. It could be a cause, a mission, or even a spiritual belief. Having a purpose gives your life direction and meaning, and it helps you endure the challenges that will inevitably come your way.

Believe in Something Greater: Define Your Purpose

As Viktor Frankl, a Holocaust survivor and renowned psychiatrist, said:

> **"Those who have a 'why' to live can bear almost any 'how'."**

When you define your purpose, it becomes your guiding light. It doesn't matter how big or small it is; it matters that it drives you. Whether you're motivated to make the world a better place or simply to be the best version of yourself, believing in something greater will keep you grounded and inspired.

Could it be that the most profound question we can ask is: should I procreate? What else matters in the grand scheme of things? This question challenges us to think about legacy, the continuation of life, and the responsibility we hold toward future generations. It's a reminder that our actions today shape the world of tomorrow. Life itself is the most sacred of all things.

At the core of the human spirit lies something far more profound than we often realise. In ancient languages, the word *spirit* itself means breath—the very essence of life that sustains us. It is this breath—this spirit—that fuels not just our physical being, but also our intuition, motivation, and drive. When we feel lost or when life doesn't seem to make sense, it's often our spirit that keeps us moving forward. Our spirit, like breath, is unseen yet essential; it guides us to keep choosing goodness and perseverance over quitting or surrendering to doubt. I am interested to know what you will choose to believe in?

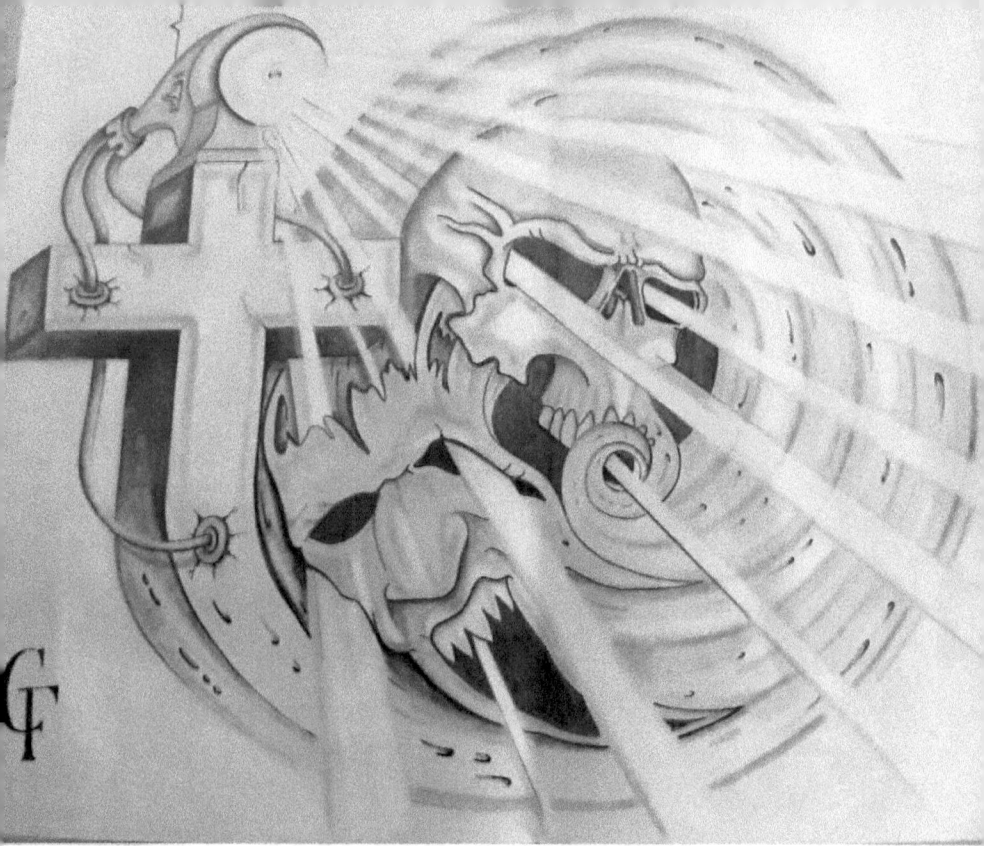

The Greeks had a concept called *Kairos*, which refers to the 'right or opportune moment'; a critical time when everything aligns perfectly for action. It's not about chronological time, but the perfect timing where destiny and opportunity meet. The image above tells a story of light working with Kairos (t) to transcend death and fear (the faces). Often, our body senses these moments before our minds can grasp them. It's that subtle intuition, that gut feeling, telling you to act, even when logic can't fully explain why. So, are you listening to your body? The worst thing I ever did in my life was stop listening to my body. I didn't even realised I had stopped until my reflux had burned a hole in my throat and I was 20kg overweight. Situations can also occur when you need to find something extra and absolutely take control of your emotion, this is when you can channel something from deep within that often doesn't actually feel like it's from you, something that feels like a guardian angel or spirit animal. This idea goes against the idea that we should always be our self, but you cannot actually be anyone else. So, go ahead and channel a bear at the gym, Einstein in the classroom, dolphin in the pool or tiger in the bedroom. Have fun with it and teach the children around you to do the same. I.e. who can be the cheekiest monkey or fastest dingo?

When striving to achieve your best, you'll quickly realise that timing is everything. The intricate role of timing in our daily lives forms the foundation of who we are and what we accomplish. Whether it's a personal goal, a professional endeavour, or a simple decision, timing is a crucial element that deserves recognition and thoughtful consideration.

Our lives are marked by moments of Kairos: the right or opportune moments where our destiny meets our choices. When we preserve these memories and recognise the significance of certain experiences, they become pillars of our personal legacy. These moments not only shape our lives but remind us of the responsibility we carry to build a life of purpose, for ourselves and those who come after us. Think of your purpose as your GPS locator, which lends itself to your moral compass. When life's messy or tough to figure out, it's what'll keep you on track and moving forward.

Sometimes, the path we're on seems unclear, and the answers we seek aren't given to us immediately. But the human spirit knows something deeper. It drives us toward purpose, urging us to take the leap of faith when the time is right. As Bob Marley once said: **"You never know how strong you are until being strong is your only choice."**

Upgrade Your Power: The Truth About Attracting Success

It's our spirit that reveals this strength, urging us to embrace Kairos—to recognise that life's most meaningful moments are not always planned or predictable, but are felt and acted upon when we are in tune with our spirit. For me, when this feeling is at its peak I just want to sing and dance with people I love - nothing else matters in those moments of perfection.

When you start to observe the frequent patterns, serendipity, coincidences, and how systems work, you'll see the miraculous nature of the universe's design; an array of symmetrical systems, like cogs and pulleys on a machine that you are privileged to observe. This perspective allows you to appreciate the complexity of life and the deeper connections that guide us. Having faith in the components that you cannot see is where we start to believe in something bigger than ourselves. It's important to trust, but I never put my faith in men to do the right thing always... I only ever trust in God or myself;

We seem to have external authorities in this world, but who really is an authority when you can think for yourself in positive ways?

Sometimes I have this overwhelming feeling throughout my body, and it doesn't feel like I have a choice, like it is some higher power controlling my decisions. Sometimes I could see this energy in others, and I would not respond to the persons words or behaviours but to their spirit and their skin, eyes, aura and discern what that need to hear so they could heal or be inspired. I suppose this is called intuition. I relate it to my gift from God. A few people around me can see what I do and often comment that they are amazed that I can do this. After working in the school system for a decade I got burnt-out doing this and my ability become reduced. It was quite mystical and highly enjoyable to read between the lines of peoples' psychology and emotions. At times when that feeling is not there, I will pause and hope it arrives. Then, if it does not I will consider if I "need" to make a decision or if I can withhold my thoughts until I am certain, if I am pressured to decide I will default to the best outcome for the most people based on all information available to me at the time, including listening to as many perspectives as possible. If I am rushed to make a decision then I remind myself that there are no wrong answers because I have faith everything will turn out exactly as it should, quite often I will ask people for a moment to think, that's easy right? But, it is always my decision in the end, which I am then responsible for, accountable for and I take ownership of. There is an old S.A.S. soldier acronym I was taught recently, "B.E.D." and "O.A.R." – Stay away from the B.E.D. (Blame - Excuse - Denial) and use the O.A.R. (Ownership - Accountability - Responsibility) to paddle your way through life. This is a good one to remember.

I keep most of my thoughts to myself and deal with my troubles, refine my dreams and articulate my day-to-day needs in prayer. I let my results be my voice to the outside world. This is a sentiment offered by dozens of wise people throughout history.

Just because you believe the world should be a certain way doesn't mean it ever will be that way. Perhaps you struggle to understand the flaws of our civilisation, there are many, but this means that humanity is still working through its collective and systemic traumas. Throughout history, figures like Buddha, Jesus, Muhammad, and countless artists, scholars, revolutionaries, and even bankers, have tried to bring their version of peace to the world. Yet, none have fully succeeded. Because we have such a traumatic backstory that we are yet to overcome.

What does peace on Earth look like? Goodness will not prevail unless we build a system that fosters prosperity for all, protecting those who seek a better world from those who intentionally oppose widespread peace. People like David Suzuki, Jacque Fresco and Buckminster Fuller are well worth reading about as they have worked extensively in an attempt to provide models for world peace, but their plans always fell on deaf ears. One day, the world may become a place of true peace and prosperity; after all, this is our responsibility to ourselves and to the Earth. Our duty! There may be something better beyond this life, but until we know, let's make the absolute most of the miracles we have before us.

Besides if we are always seeking "better" and "more" we will inevitably end up missing all the great parts of living. All the little destinations along the way to be experienced and cherished. It certainly pays to be present in the moment, but spend some time thinking back of the joys that has been or dream about what could be. It doesn't have to be "better" or "more" it could be "different" or "new."

Mini Challenge:
Personal Purpose Statement

Craft a personal mission statement reflecting your core values and goals. Keep it visible for a week and reflect on how it influences your decisions and priorities. Journal on how clarity of purpose helps guide your actions.

How did crafting a purpose statement help clarify what truly matters to you? Reflect on how this sense of purpose could guide your actions and bring deeper meaning to your daily experiences:

_____
_____
_____
_____

Chapter 9:
Work Ethic and Creating Passive Income

Living with purpose is essential, but so is creating a life where you have the freedom to pursue that purpose. Financial independence gives you the time and space to focus on what truly matters. Building a strong work ethic and creating passive income streams are the keys to achieving this freedom.

You've probably heard the phrase 'work smarter, not harder,' but let's break that down. Having a strong work ethic means being dedicated, focused, and disciplined when you work. But it doesn't mean working yourself into exhaustion. Passive income means earning money while you sleep, freeing up time and mental space for creativity and personal growth.

Napoleon Hill, the author of 'Think and Grow Rich,' said it best:

> **"Whatever the mind can conceive and believe, it can achieve."**

Whether you're flipping items for a quick profit or building long-term income streams, your mindset is the most important asset. Passive income is not just about financial freedom, but about building the kind of life where you are in control of your time and future. That's what makes you powerful. CONTROL! When you can switch something on or off, make it hot or cold, wet or dry, fast or slow, rich or poor, alive or dead… these things give you control – doesn't that feel powerful? Money can achieve these things, but with control comes great responsibility… Firstly, who is currently in control of you and your surroundings? Now, how much control do you really want?

If you were to take over the world, how would you do things differently to the current leader and what would be the consequences of your decision. Would people be better off under your rule?

Anyway, let's remain focused on what you can currently control and see if we can build from there.

To build wealth, you must first learn how to manage the money you have. Wealth isn't just about making money; it's about using it wisely, from budgeting to strategic investing. Money changes a person… money can kill too. Temptations significantly increase when you have money, alcohol, drugs, fast cars, bikes, boats, bad investments, mixing with new people you don't know… If you received 100 million dollars in the bank today. How long would you survive? Do you know how to protect it, and yourself? There is a lot to know about serious wealth, more than just accounting, tax, banking, financial advisors and dealing with family and friends who come out of the woodworks.

Upgrade Your Power: The Truth About Attracting Success

True financial independence means having control over your life and time; freedom that enables you to pursue a life of purpose. Creating a budget is a powerful habit you can develop. It allows you to track your spending, control your expenses, and save for your future. A simple rule is this: 20% of all the money you earn is for yourself, while 80% is for all expenses and responsibilities. If you borrow money, make sure it's for something that will make you money or significantly improve your chances of a better life. All other reasons are luxuries you can live without until you can afford them with your own money. Basic debt spent wisely can be hugely beneficial when you have an investment that will make you a proven income and return on your investment. Other than that, avoid going into unnecessary debt or any debt with high interest, or with irreputable people and companies. And, always pay back your debts before their due dates. This protects your financial health and builds trust with lenders. As Napoleon Hill reminds us in *Think and Grow Rich*, wealth isn't just about making money; it's about how you manage and grow it. *The Barefoot Investor* emphasises the importance of setting up financial safety nets. Small, consistent savings and investments can grow into life-changing wealth over time. Start early, invest wisely, and let compound interest work its magic. Taking the time to make actionable smart goals will be one of the most important steps for your future.

As you work toward your goals, keep in mind that the path isn't always straightforward. Many systems, including governments and large institutions, prioritise their own interests. This means they may not always support your vision of success. For example: unnecessary taxes on fuel and income; allowing prices of utilities to skyrocket; employee wages not keeping up with inflation; the housing crisis; underregulating medicines and imported foods; inflating Council fees and permitting silly regulations that prevent people from getting ahead financially or living in better conditions because it doesn't align with local policy. Navigating these challenges requires awareness and discernment, especially when it comes to the way food, medicine, media and other policies are regulated. While you may encounter well-intentioned individuals in these systems—teachers, nurses, and first responders—it's essential to recognise that true allies are rare. Focus on surrounding yourself with those who truly care about your growth and be prepared to advocate for yourself when the system falls short. Aligning with government funding is another way to make really good money, but you will always be on the short leash of the authorities as they change regulations and policies to suit their agenda, which is always to maintain control at all costs.

When you find the good ones, treat them well and keep them in your circle; whether it's a mechanic, dentist, doctor, lawyer, hairdresser, broker, builder or accountant. My good mate is a probiotic pharmacist, and my wife is an RN; I need these people in my life to improve my chances of survival and success. Building a network of trustworthy professionals can make all the difference, not just in achieving financial freedom but in navigating the complexities of life itself.

Here are some ways you can start building income. Some are a side-hustle, others are passive income:

1. Selling digital products: Create something like an eBook, artwork, or even templates, and sell them on platforms like Etsy or Amazon. Leverage social media.

2. YouTube or TikTok: If you're passionate about a topic, create content and get paid through ad revenue once you grow a following

3. Affiliate marketing: Share product links on a blog or social media and earn a commission every time someone buys using your link.

4. Stock photography: If you like taking photos, you can sell them on sites like Shutterstock or Adobe Stock.

5. Start a blog or podcast: Create content that can eventually bring in ad revenue or sponsorships once you have an audience.

6. Investing in stocks, shares or crypto: While this takes time and a bit of research, putting money into stocks or funds can generate income as they grow. Find consistent and trustworthy people to follow and learn from them. Perhaps join a trading group.

7. Renting out items: Own something valuable like a granny flat, trailer, camera, bike, or even a gaming console. Rent it out to others for some extra cash. Ultimately building a real estate portfolio or becoming known for renting out quality items would be ideal. In fact, one of the easiest businesses to make profit is storage containers. If you have some backing and you're in the right location, you should investigate setting this up and automating the process for customers.

8. Flipping Items: This is an often overlooked, simple way to make money. You can find underpriced items at garage sales, second-hand stores, or even online, and flip them for a profit. With a little research, you can buy something at a low price and sell it for more. It teaches you how to assess value, spot opportunities, and develop an entrepreneurial mindset. Learning to be thrifty, to negotiate and haggle with people is a powerful skill we call salesmanship. When flipping items or investing in other passive income streams, always aim for ROI (Return on Investment). Spend wisely, considering whether your money will grow or work for you over time. It's always good to have an item sold before you buy it. The best items to flip are things you know something about, things that you have support with parts or repairs to fix up, and things that other people "need". You can go niche and try and flip old cars, nice boats or antiques but these are awkward and hard work unless you really know what you're doing. My favourites are gold and silver, sports shoes, box trailers, caravans, clothes, tools, fishing gear and anything else I think people want that will be little work and will sell quickly. Ultimately, I wish I had a land portfolio (houses are hard work, but land parcels are seriously good money).

9. Invent something: get your creative hat on and show the world how you can innovate and invent something useful. The bigger the problem you solve, the more money you will make.

10. Invest in yourself: Working for yourself can be highly rewarding personally and financially. Be your own boss or join a syndicate and deliver a great service/product, take care of your customers and keep quality accounting records.

I have a little bit of money to invest, if you have a great idea please send it through to me. We can chat. Investing is one of the most powerful ways to build wealth, but it also carries risks. Due diligence—the practice of thoroughly researching and analysing an investment opportunity before committing—ensures that you're making well-informed choices rather than relying on impulse or hype. By scrutinising the credibility of an investment, understanding market trends, and evaluating potential risks, you protect yourself from preventable losses. Taking time for thorough research enhances your ability to spot valuable opportunities and steer clear of pitfalls, setting you up for long-term financial growth and security. This diligence is essential, even when receiving advice from trusted friends. In all-important decision-making situations, ask the difficult questions upfront to avoid future surprises and ensure that each decision or investment aligns with your goals.

Fundamental to surviving in the later part of the 21st Century is an understanding of the AI-driven society we are heading into. Critical thinking and digital literacy will become vital in the new tech-centric world that is on our doorstep. This is the moment when your due diligence is a powerful habit to develop.

This same commitment to diligence and follow-through applies to personal endeavours. It's easy to be inspired at the start, but true accomplishment comes from completing what you set out to do. Finishing your projects not only creates something tangible and valuable; it also strengthens your reputation as someone who brings ideas to life with discipline and reliability. When you complete what you start, you have created a product, something tangible that holds worth in the world. Even more, by consistently finishing what you start, you transform yourself into a product of value. You become someone known for your discipline, your reliability, and your ability to bring ideas to life. As you continue to finish your projects, you build credibility and respect in your personal and professional life. Success comes to those who can communicate effectively, turn effort into results and trade their time for purposeful outcomes, especially if it makes someone else's life easier, empowered or wealthy.

When faced with something you don't enjoy doing, don't run from it; find something within the task that makes it interesting, rewarding, or joyful. Redefining the term 'work' to be associated with happiness and joyful is a secret to a good life. This is what winners are made from: trying, putting in effort, and discovering meaning even in the difficult parts of life. Complaining about life's challenges is for losers. Instead, embrace the hard parts and learn from them. This is work ethic!

Mini Challenge:
Vision Board Creation

Create a vision board representing your financial and career aspirations. Place it in a space where you'll see it daily. For the next week, reflect on how these goals influence your motivation and focus for building a life of freedom and purpose.

What new possibilities for income or productivity did you discover, and how could they shape your future? Reflect on how building financial independence and a strong work ethic could open up new choices and freedoms:

_____
_____
_____
_____

Conclusion: Your Journey to Power

Attracting powerful people isn't about pretending to be someone you're not. True power comes from embracing and amplifying your authentic self: the best version of you. It's about becoming someone who naturally draws others in, not through force or manipulation, but through your undeniable presence, spirit, talent and character that it takes to continue to grow beyond the pages of this booklet.

By refining your hygiene, mastering your voice, sharpening your listening skills, surrounding yourself with a proactive network, and developing your unique talents and confidence, you build a magnetic presence that can't be ignored. The world respects those who respect themselves, and as you invest in these areas of your life, you'll notice something powerful: people will begin to gravitate toward you, not just because of what you do, but because of who you are.

Maya Angelou once said:

> "People will forget what you said, people will forget what you did, but people will never forget how you made them feel."

Upgrade Your Power: The Truth About Attracting Success

It's not just the words you speak or the actions you take that make the impact—it's the energy you bring into every interaction. And as Bruce Lee so wisely put it:

> **"Don't think. Feel."**

Sometimes, we over-analyse or second-guess ourselves, but true power comes from trusting your instincts and letting your presence and energy flow naturally. Feeling the moment, rather than thinking about it, helps you act with authenticity and draw people in effortlessly.

The journey to power is not a quick fix or a one-time effort; it's a lifelong commitment to growth, self-awareness, and the constant pursuit of excellence. Sifting through the infinite knowledge available today is one of life's great difficulties. We live in a world with endless access to information, but navigating through what is helpful, truthful, or aligned with your purpose is the real challenge. It's through this careful process of discernment that you find the path to living your best life.

As you continue to invest in yourself, the world will start to take notice. Opportunities will present themselves, the right people will enter your life, and the doors to success will begin to open.

Conclusion: Your Journey to Power

You know, if I had to give up all the control, money, power and all I got in return was safe place to live, a good character and wonderful people to be with, I would do that in a heartbeat. Having great people in our lives is hands down the most important achievement in a person's life.

My mates often say something like: He who has the most toys may have a lot of fun, but he who has the most people turn up to their funeral certainly had the best life.

Your journey to power starts today. Every decision you make, every step you take, leads you closer to the empowered, successful individual you were always meant to be. So don't hold back. Start now. Invest in yourself and watch as the world shifts to meet your ambitions. The future is yours to shape—take it, own it, and rise to your highest potential. I pray this booklet has helped you on your journey to your full potential. Don't let anyone tell you that reaching your full potential isn't a destination—it absolutely is. As Shakespeare said:

> **"All the world's a stage, and all the men and women merely players."**

Upgrade Your Power: The Truth About Attracting Success

Conclusion: Your Journey to Power

So, what role will you play in this remarkable performance we call life?

For me, I am filled with love but short on time…

Take what you've learned here and apply it, knowing that the real work begins now, as you continue to sift through knowledge, hone your skills, **try** to be the best you can be in any given moment and become the powerful person you are meant to be.

Feel the energy within…
Now that you have all the philosophy, the entrepreneurial techniques, and the networking capacity, you can make life happen by your design. The tools are in your hands, and the possibilities are endless. If you ever feel stuck, don't hesitate to reach out. I'll try to help—**Mr. James Fuller, The Teacher**—and together we can continue this journey defining your success. This booklet is written as a simplistic gateway to my next books, I hope you will accompany me on this journey.

Now, go back and read all your highlighted sections, this will consolidate everything you have read … you won't regret it. **Keep it real everyone!**

13 Books Recommended for Personal Development

1. **The Tao of Jeet Kune Do** by Bruce Lee
2. **Meditations** by Marcus Aurelius
3. **The Way of the Peaceful Warrior** by Dan Millman
4. **Think and Grow Rich** by Napoleon Hill
5. **How to Win Friends and Influence People** by Dale Carnegie
6. **The 7 Habits of Highly Effective People** by Stephen Covey
7. **Body Language** by Allan Pease
8. **Tao Te Ching** by Lao Tzu
9. **War and Peace** by Leo Tolstoy
10. **The Kingdom of God is Within You** by Leo Tolstoy
11. **The Sermon on the Mount** by Jesus Christ
12. **Atomic Habits** by James Clear
13. **Flow: The Psychology of Optimal Experience** by Mihaly Csikszentmihalyi

Conclusion: Your Journey to Power

Powerful Terms for you to ponder:
(Some that you may not find on Google)

Specialised:

Biomimicry in daily life
Negentropic being
Triggerpoint psychology
Looping theory
Mirrormind
iSpirit Achievement Matrix
Zone of Proximal Development
Flow
Entropy

General:

Necessity
Enough
Expectation
Work
Technique
Strategy
Love
Empathy
Peace of mind

NOTES

NOTES

NOTES

www.ingramcontent.com/pod-product-compliance
Lightning Source LLC
Chambersburg PA
CBHW061743070526
44585CB00024B/2786